# NAOMI

## SEASON ONE

# NAOMI
## SEASON ONE

**BRIAN MICHAEL BENDIS**
**DAVID F. WALKER**
writers

**JAMAL CAMPBELL**
artist

**JOSH REED**
**CARLOS M. MANGUAL**
letterers

**JAMAL CAMPBELL**
collection and original series cover artist

NAOMI created by BENDIS, WALKER, and CAMPBELL

SUPERMAN created by JERRY SIEGEL and JOE SHUSTER
By special arrangement with the Jerry Siegel family

**MIKE COTTON, ANDY KHOURI** Editors – Original Series
**JESSICA CHEN** Associate Editor – Original Series
**SCOTT NYBAKKEN** Editor – Collected Edition
**STEVE COOK** Design Director – Books
**CURTIS KING JR.** Publication Design
**ERIN VANOVER** Publication Production

**MARIE JAVINS** Editor-in-Chief, DC Comics

**DANIEL CHERRY III** Senior VP – General Manager
**JIM LEE** Publisher & Chief Creative Officer
**JOEN CHOE** VP – Global Brand & Creative Services
**DON FALLETTI** VP – Manufacturing Operations & Workflow Management
**LAWRENCE GANEM** VP – Talent Services
**ALISON GILL** Senior VP – Manufacturing & Operations
**NICK J. NAPOLITANO** VP – Manufacturing Administration & Design
**NANCY SPEARS** VP – Revenue

**NAOMI: SEASON ONE**

DC Comics, 2900 West Alameda Ave., Burbank, CA 91505
Printed by LSC Communications, Owensville, MO, USA. 11/26/21.
First Printing. ISBN: 978-1-77951-639-8

Library of Congress
Cataloging-in-Publication Data is available.

DC COMICS PROUDLY PRESENTS

# NAOMI

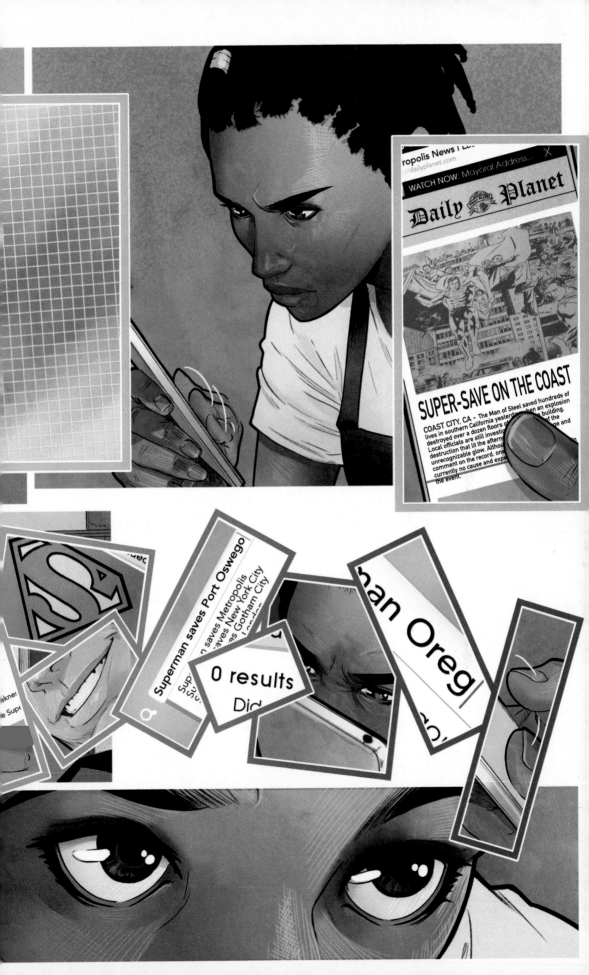

WATCH NOW: Mayoral Address...

# Daily Planet

## SUPER-SAVE ON THE COAST

COAST CITY, CA - The Man of Steel saved hundreds of lives in southern California yesterday when an explosion destroyed over a dozen floors of a building. Local officials are still investigating the cause of the destruction that lit the afternoon sky with a strange and unrecognizable glow. Although one comment on the record, one currently no cause and expe the event.

Superman saves Port Oswego

saves Metropolis
saves New York City
saves Gotham City

0 results

Did

han Oreg

Dee.

Next: MEET THE PARENTS

Please...

...I came in here and asked you when the last time some crazy superhero hit Port Oswego...

...and then *you* say it happened seventeen years ago on March fourteenth...

...and *that's* the date I was adopted.

Dee, you're—you're, no offense, the town mechanic.

We've never *actually* spoken before...

...how do you even *know* what day I was adopted?

"I'm so mad at you."

TAK TAK TAK TAK TAK

THREE

...that is our way.

"Qyeala was mission leader. I was part of her team.

"You would call it.

"We were the most elite secret force in the Thanagarian Command.

"We would go from planet system to planet system on different covert missions. Sometimes in—you call it 'undercover.'

"Rescue missions, extractions, strikes.

"Special types of missions for our special abilities.

Next:
**The Beginning**

"So when high command ordered me to go to Earth, undercover, to track a missing black guard Thanagarian assassin...

"I was honored.

"After the things I'd seen and done, the offer of a simple fact-finding mission on some simple planet without even a shred of orbital mechanics...

"It sounded *fantastic!*"

"But they never ever called.

"I don't know if the war went sideways or we had new leadership or they just plain forgot about us...

"But no one came looking for me.

"Or Dee."

"And *Mom?*

"You weren't, like, I don't know, completely and totally freaked out that Dad's an alien from outer space?"

"Uh, nope."

"Mom!"

"Hey! What can I tell you?"

"And, Dad, you just *told* her?"

"Of course. I was *madly* in love with her.

"Why would I keep that from her?"

Next: NAOMI REVEALED

"They found me—my adopted parents found me as a baby.

"My dad and *Dee* literally found me on the high school football field—

"Involved in some crazy space war stuff they couldn't understand—They never understood.

"But my parents and Dee, who do not care for each other, kept it to themselves as part of all the alien secrets they keep.

"And all that was swaddled with me was this little, I guess, black box thing.

"But it wasn't made of anything I ever felt before.

"And when I touched it.

"When I put it in the palm of my hand.

"It—it *dissolved* inside me. It didn't hurt.

"My skin was tingling. My heart was—*ugh!*

"And then...

"There was a voice.

"It was—at first I thought it was *my* voice."

I AM TOLD WHAT YOU ARE EXPERIENCING RIGHT NOW...IS *UNIQUE.*

MY VOICE IN YOUR HEAD.

"It sounded exactly like my voice when I hear it played back.

"And then it—I realized it was the voice of..."

MY THOUGHTS—BEING SENT DIRECTLY TO YOU.

OH, MY DAUGHTER.

MY BABY GIRL.

AT THE TIME I AM RECORDING THIS MESSAGE TO YOU, YOU ARE STILL A NEWBORN BABY.

I AM LOOKING RIGHT AT YOUR GORGEOUS BABY BROWN EYES AS I DO THIS.

I HOPE YOU CAN *FEEL* HOW MUCH I LOVE YOU.

WHAT I AM GOING TO TELL YOU, I AM TOLD, IS SOMETHING NO ONE ON YOUR WORLD KNOWS ABOUT.

"BY THE TIME YOU GET THIS, MAYBE THEY WILL.

"I HOPE THEY DO KNOW OF US. I HOPE IT INSPIRES YOU TO TAKE WHAT I AM SAYING VERY SERIOUSLY.

"I'M NOT AN EXPERT IN **ANY** OF THIS BY **ANY** MEANS. IT HAD TO BE EXPLAINED TO ME AND NOW I AM EXPLAINING IT TO YOU.

"OTHER EARTHS.

"I DON'T KNOW HOW MANY THERE ARE BUT I HAVE BEEN TOLD BY SOMEONE WHO KNOWS THAT THERE ARE A FEW.

"AND THE ONE YOU HAVE GROWN UP ON IS **VERY** SIMILAR TO THE ONE YOU WERE BORN TO.

"BUT THE BIGGEST DIFFERENCE BETWEEN THE TWO EARTHS IS SOMETHING WE CALL **THE CRISIS.**

"YEARS AGO, FROM ABUSE AND NEGLECT, THE NATURAL PROTECTIVE LAYERS THAT SURROUNDED EARTH COLLAPSED.

"WE WERE ALL WARNED IT COULD HAPPEN. OVER AND OVER. FOR YEARS.

"THOSE WHO WERE IN CHARGE OF DECIDING SUCH THINGS CHOSE TO IGNORE THE WARNINGS.

"**BUT** WHEN THE OZONE LAYER FELL, WE DISCOVERED, AFTER THE FACT, IT WAS JUST ONE OF A HANDFUL OF LAYERS THAT DISAPPEARED THAT DAY.

"WE DIDN'T HAVE THE SCIENCE TO UNDERSTAND WHAT WE WERE DOING TO THE EARTH AND HOW MUCH IT WAS PROTECTING US FROM THINGS WE COULD NOT CONTROL.

"ON THAT DAY NEW RADIATIONS/ENERGIES BATHED **THE ENTIRE WORLD.**

"RADIATIONS THAT AGAIN, SCIENCE DIDN'T EVEN KNOW EXISTED.

"THE CRISIS ITSELF ONLY LASTED A MINUTE...

"BUT WHEN IT WAS OVER...OUR WORLD WAS FOREVER CHANGED."

"ONE MONTH AFTER **THE CRISIS**, FOURTEEN OF US WERE KILLED IN BATTLE BY THE OTHERS.

"OF THE FIFTEEN SURVIVORS, SEVEN JUST UP AND LEFT THE EARTH IN DISGUST.

"AND NEVER CAME BACK.

"THE EIGHT OF US THAT STAYED...

"WE WERE ABLE TO CALL A TRUCE JUST BEFORE THE ENTIRE EARTH BURNED TO ASH.

"JUST.

"THE WORST OF US IS A MONSTER NAMED **ZUMBADO**.

"ON THE DAY OF THE CRISIS HE WAS ON HIS WAY TO THE ELECTRIC CHAIR FOR MASS MURDER.

"OF ALL THE PEOPLE IN THE WORLD. A TERRIBLE BROKEN PERSON WAS GIVEN THE POWER OF A GOD."

"WE COULDN'T STOP HIM FROM TURNING HALF THE WORLD INTO THE WORST VERSION OF ITSELF-- WE COULDN'T STOP HIM FROM RULING OVER IT.

"AFTER HE TORE THROUGH THE WORLD, WE HAD TO CARVE OUT AND FIGHT FOR SECTIONS OF THE ENTIRE PLANET AND DECLARE IT **OURS.**

"HE FORCED US TO BECOME RULERS--KINGS AND QUEENS.

"I, WE ARE SO FRUSTRATED BY WHAT HE IS DOING.

"HE'S DESTROYING THE WORLD IN SELFISHNESS AND GREED FASTER THAN ANYBODY ELSE EVER COULD.

"HE CAN'T SEE FIVE FEET IN FRONT OF HIMSELF.

"WITH EVERY BATTLE HE GOBBLES UP NATURAL RESOURCES THAT WE JUST DON'T HAVE ANYMORE.

"BUT HE THINKS THIS POWER WAS GIVEN TO HIM FOR A REASON AND THAT REASON WAS $@#$@ EVERYONE.

"YOUR FATHER AND I WAKE UP EVERY MORNING WONDERING IF **THIS** IS THE DAY HE'S JUST GOING TO DECIDE TO ATTACK US.

"HE GOES IN FRONT OF **HIS PEOPLE** AND TALKS ABOUT IT. HE RILES THEM UP WITH THE IDEA OF BATHING IN OUR BLOOD.

"BUT HE HAS CONQUERED SO MUCH. HE HAS SO MANY OF HIS DESIRES MET...

"THAT IT KEEPS HIM BUSY.

"BUT THERE IS ALWAYS THAT WORRY ABOUT **THE BALANCE.**

"ABOUT ONE OF US STEPPING OVER THE IMAGINARY LINE IN **HIS** HEAD.

"AND JUST SO YOU KNOW, SWEETIE, I WAS A SCHOOLTEACHER."

"AND THEN ONE DAY I WOKE UP AND FOUND MYSELF LIKE THIS--IN-IN **CONSTANT** BATTLE. YOUR FATHER, YOUR FATHER IS ONE OF THE DAMN GOOD ONES. THEY **ARE** OUT THERE. A GOOD MAN WHO HAS BEEN FORCED TO MAKE SOME TERRIBLE CHOICES. LIKE ME, FORCED INTO THIS ROLE AS PROTECTOR. BECAUSE IF NOT US, WHO? WE FOUND EACH OTHER ON THE BATTLEFIELD. YOUR FATHER WAS A GAMING SOFTWARE ENGINEER. HE KNEW STRATEGY GAMES AND **THAT** MADE HIM AN OUTSTANDING WARTIME TACTICIAN IN THE REAL WORLD. YOUR DAD'S INTELLIGENCE AND JUST GENERAL ZEST FOR LIFE DRIVES ZUMBADO INSANE. BUT LET'S TALK ABOUT YOU: SINCE **THE CRISIS** NONE OF OUR KIND WERE ABLE TO PROCREATE. WITH EACH OTHER OR WITH **THE NORMALS.** I HOPE YOU'RE OLD ENOUGH TO KNOW WHAT I'M TALKING ABOUT. WE WEREN'T SURE WHAT IT MEANT FOR OUR FUTURE...UNTIL US.

"UNTIL YOU.

"YOU CAME ALONG--THE FIRST BORN OF THE CRISIS. THE PURE-BLOOD POWER. AND IF YOU ARE HEARING THIS RECORDING, THEN OUR FRIEND **AKIRA** WAS RIGHT. ZUMBADO FLIPPED OUT WHEN HE HEARD WORD OF YOUR EXISTENCE. HE CAME TO KILL YOU TO PROVE HIS SUPERIORITY. BUT **WE** HAVE SOMETHING HE DOES NOT...FRIENDS. THAT'S WHERE YOUR AUNTIE AKIRA, ONE OF US, COMES IN. HER POWER IS A SUPER-INTELLECT. AKIRA WAS ALWAYS BRILLIANT. THE CRISIS MADE HER JUST MORE BRILLIANT. SHE IS THE REASON YOU ARE GETTING THIS MESSAGE. SHE IS THE REASON YOU'RE SAFE. SHE'S THE REASON YOU WERE ABLE TO LIVE AMONG THE REGULAR PEOPLE UNTIL NOW.

"IF YOU'RE HEARING THIS, WE ARE ALL MOST PROBABLY LONG DEAD. THAT IS THE **ONLY** REASON WE WOULD **EVER** SEND YOU AWAY. BECAUSE YOU WERE IN DANGER. IT WAS AKIRA'S IDEA TO SEND YOU AWAY TO AN EARTH THAT COULD HANDLE WHATEVER YOU TURN INTO. A PLACE ZUMBADO WOULD NEVER BE ABLE TO FIND.

"AKIRA SAYS IF YOU DO HAVE SPECIAL POWERS, LIKE US, THE WORLD YOU HAVE BEEN SENT TO CAN HANDLE IT. IF YOU ARE GETTING THIS...I DIDN'T WANT ANY OF THIS. WE INSTRUCTED OUR VERY LOYAL FRIENDS TO GET YOU TO THIS NEW EARTH AND FIND YOU A FAMILY WITH POWERS WHILE WE HOLD BACK ZUMBADO. TELL YOUR ADOPTED PARENTS, THE NEW FAMILY YOU FOUND, THAT WE SHARE A LOVE STRONGER THAN I CAN EXPRESS. ACROSS ENTIRE WORLDS.

"WOW."

Get it together!

Where is Naomi?!

You can do this!

Calm yourself. Breathe, focus!

She— she told me what happened! She told me about the cave!

Good. So you know.

That— that helps us.

You're an alien from outer effin' space!

Where were YOU when Ugly McFugly showed up out of nowhere?!

"Out of nowhere" where?

What happened?

Where is she?

We don't know, Dee!

A lot has happened.

Where is she?!

And you're here to—?

Help you.

Right.

**There** she is! Good call, Greg!

Annabelle! **WHERE'S NAOMI?**

**TOO MUCH!**

This is— it's just—

*It's just*—

I **so** tried to stop her, but...

Annabelle!

Okay, so, my best friend was just telling me how she is a super-person not from this Earth...when there was a-a-a flashy light—

Flashy light where? Annabelle, be more specific.

There—there was a **bright light,** like, right there!

There really was one!

And he just kind of came **through** it.

He?

Ugly McFugly?

**VROOOOOM**

You, silly one.

What's happened to Naomi?

Oh, okay. Now **you're** here...

It was **right here**...

A— a whole world!

A window, like, into another entire world...

# AFTERWORD

Hi! I'm Brian Bendis. I'm one of the co-creators of *Naomi*, and I am writing this afterword behind my fellow co-creators' backs. As I type, neither David nor Jamal know that I'm writing this. I just wanted a little me-and-you time to talk about...them.

So David and I have been friends for a long time. When the Bendi first moved to Portland in the early 2000s, David and I met and quickly became friends. I was already reading his often-awesome underground blaxploitation zine *BadAzz MoFo*, as it had made its way to a record store that I frequented back in Cleveland. (In the '90s there were record stores that you could frequent. Check out the movie *High Fidelity*. It was just like that.)

In Portland, David was the local movie reviewer for the free rock 'n' roll newspaper. David would often invite me to the advance screenings with him. We had a lot of fun, and from there we built our friendship on a shared love of story and craft. I talk about this publicly anywhere I can, but David was a big part of the success of Miles Morales. David was a helping hand and a kind and honest sounding board. The pop culture phenomenon of Miles is because of David's generous help and honesty.

From there, I eventually asked him to come teach with me. I had been teaching college writing for a few years, but with the growing number of children in my house and the shocking developments with some of my comics being turned into TV shows and movies, I was worried I wasn't always going to make it to class. As David and I were so similar in temperament and passion about certain things, I thought he would be an excellent pinch hitter. (Also, writers need to get out of the house.)

As the years passed, the class became less about each of us tag-team teaching and more about two nerdy professors in a classroom holding court together.

It was during these sessions that David and I dug deeper into the structure of the hero's journey and the evolving modern version of it. I would look across the classroom and see David and think to myself, "He and I should be doing this, not just talking about it."

I had warned him that we were going to create something together.

Then I got this sweet deal at DC. And then I got real sick and almost went away. I don't love discussing this next part, but it's true, and it's a big part of the emotions on the pages you JUST read. Over a year ago I got really sick and I was told I wasn't gonna get better. David, like my other best friends, was right there. Right there.

It was during these hospital visits that we had the earliest discussions about what *Naomi* would be. David and I were going to create a character together that would reflect a lot of the truth of his growing up in Portland while at the same time speaking to the DC Universe in a new and exciting way. We didn't know her name or her powers, but we knew...*why*. Creating new things is REALLY hard, but knowing *why* early on is really...special. I sat in the hospital with the knowledge that I was never going to meet Naomi, and David was at my bedside as often as humanly possible.

But hey! Things kind of miraculously went the other way, and the very next week *Naomi* was born.

What I'm saying is, this book came out of...a lot of emotions. This book came out of a newfound lease on life and a newfound level of friendship and partnership that we didn't even know we had. And a lot of feelings about family!

Sorry to get so personal and emotional, but everything about creating *Naomi* was personal and emotional.

BUT! As well as I personally know David, that's as *little* as I still know Jamal—I know absolutely nothing about him other than there is nothing you can't throw at him. There is no panel or page he won't bring truth to. Jamal had some amazing choices in front of him, and he chose *Naomi*. In return, we did everything we could to make Naomi's journey something worth Jamal's immense talent. Thank you, Jamal!

Some of you might know that I have two adopted daughters. *Naomi* is not a direct reflection of them. Like other subjects in life, when you have something like adoption in your family, you might find yourself lucky enough to be surrounded by other families with their own similar but different stories and energies. Almost everyone involved in this book has a very special type of family.

So no, this story is not my daughters' story in disguise. My daughters know their stories and they can tell their stories one day in whatever shape or form they want. But the truth of adoption, the universal shared truth, has been such a big part of all of our lives that we wanted *Naomi* to be able to reflect it in a fun, true way. Of course, there have been so many orphans in comics. (What do Bruce Wayne, Clark Kent, and Peter Parker all have in common?) Naomi fits into a long tradition, but from her own unique family and perspective.

My daughter Sabrina did double-check about my human upbringing. It was a fair ask.

Although this is not the story of my daughters, they have spent a great deal of time discussing and building *Naomi* with us. They feel their connection to her. It was my daughter Tabatha who, having seen Jamal's first images of Naomi, pointed to me and said, "Thor!" I said, "What does that mean?" She replied, "How people feel when Thor walks in the room is how they should feel about Naomi." The end.

The fact is, *Naomi* became a major DC powerhouse because...yeah. Tabatha was right.

By now, David, Jamal, and I have had quite a few months of this book's runaway success to deal with, and we still haven't been able to process it. Multiple printings? Wow! We will never fully understand it other than realizing that we've had that great experience of loving something while doing it and then having the audience respond accordingly.

What an amazing experience this has been. I'm so glad we got to share this with you on numerous levels.

Please share this book with somebody who needs to spend some time with Naomi. That's why we made her. That's why she's here.

Thank you.

And hey, you know what's better than saying, "Welcome to *Naomi*!"?

Saying, "See you for Season Two!"

**BENDIS!**
Portland, Oregon | 2019

NAOMI    ANNABELLE    SOOZE    FELICITY    DUANG    ANTHONY    HILLARY    RUTH

DORMANT

Active

NATHAN     BRYCE     COLLEEN     DR. ABBY     PETE     D.

NAOMI